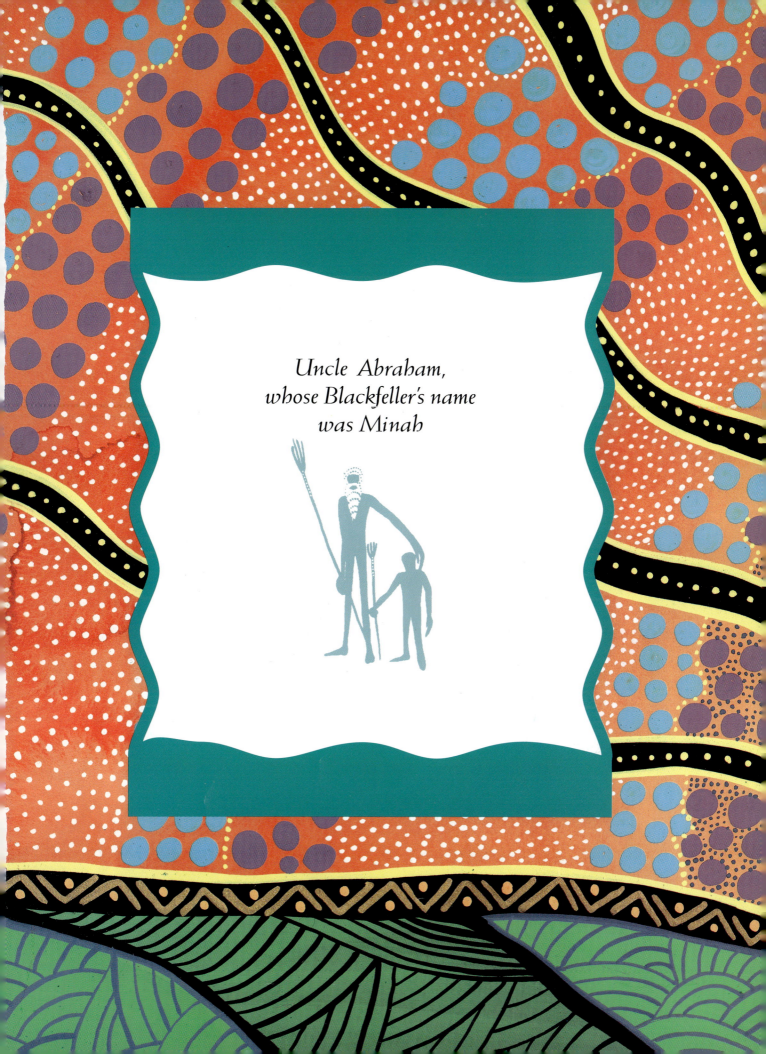

Uncle Abraham, whose Blackfeller's name was Minah

With thanks to Tracey Leanne ~ Bronwyn

An Angus & Robertson Publication

Angus&Robertson, an imprint of
HarperCollins*Publishers*
25 Ryde Road, Pymble, Sydney NSW 2073, Australia
31 View Road, Glenfield, Auckland 10, New Zealand

First published in *The Nearest the White Man Gets*
by Hale & Iremonger in 1989
This edition first published in Australia in 1995

Original story collected from Percy Mumbulla
by Roland Robinson, text copyright © Estate of Roland Robinson 1989, 1995
Illustrations copyright © Bronwyn Bancroft 1995

This book is copyright.
Apart from any fair dealing for the purposes of private study, research, criticism or review, as permitted under the Copyright Act, no part may be reproduced by any process without written permission. Inquiries should be addressed to the publishers.

National Library of Australia
Cataloguing-in-Publication data:

Mumbulla, Percy.
　Minah.
　ISBN 0 207 18483 6.

　[1.] Aborigines, Australian - New South Wales - Poetry.
　I. Robinson, Roland, 1912-1992. II. Bancroft, Bronwyn.
　III. Title.
A821.3

Printed in Hong Kong

7 6 5 4 3 2 1
99 98 97 96 95

Minah

A POEM IN FOUR PARTS

Collected by
Roland Robinson

Related by
Percy Mumbulla

Illustrated by
Bronwyn Bancroft

Angus&Robertson
An imprint of HarperCollinsPublishers

ONE

Guneena

Every time I lie down alongside a river
and hear the wind in the oaks
it puts me in mind of my poor old grand-uncle Minah.

My old grand-uncle was lying down under the oaks
and he was dying. My old dad was with him.
My old dad could feel these things.
He had that power.

He said, 'I think I'll shift you.
I don't like it here.
There's something going to happen.'

GUNEENA

He shifted old uncle Minah,
put the tent-sticks in another place.
It wasn't very long before a big limb broke off
and fell down and stuck in the ground
where my grand-uncle had been lying.

And my old father brought him back to die
at Wallaga Lake.

He'd been caught with the *guneena*,
the devil's stones.

✦ GUNEENA ✦

When I'm lying down under these oaks
down at Bega
I used to think about poor old uncle Minah.
He used to put his arms round me and say,
'My great-great-grandchildren.'

I was his favourite.
I was like a little poddy calf,
a little fat-belly feller, you might say.
I was never with the young fellers.

✧ GUNEENA ✧

I followed the old people.

They would hunt me back,
I would cry and they would take me up
and put me on their shoulders.
I used to sit down and listen
to the old people yarning.

But these young fellers, they don't realise.
They'd laugh at you.
They say, 'Ar, he's a *burra*, a liar.
He couldn't catch a dorg with such things.'

But those things did happen.

TWO

Marrung

Whenever I used to see one of those old fellers
going off with a spear for *marrung* — fish —
I'd watch him. I'd run after him.

The old lad would crouch right down with his spear.
He'd make a faint move to frighten the fish.
When the fish didn't move
he'd drive the spear right into him.
He'd have that fish shaking on his spear.

✧ MARRUNG ✧

I was only a little feller
but I had that sense to follow
and learn how to do all those things.
That's why I don't use a line for my fish.
I use my fish-spear;
my father taught me how to make them.

MARRUNG

I can use the woomera
and the spear with two barbs.

MARRUNG

I can make a boomerang
to go whistling like a duck
and come back,
right back to my foot.

◆ MARRUNG ◆

Every time I come to a river like this
and hear the wind in those she-oaks
I sit down and those times come back to me.

I can see my old great-uncle Minah lying down.
He had a long white smoky beard, *walloo* we call it,
and his hair, *jirral*, was smoke-dried, white.

He was lying down and looking at the sky
and must have been saying in his own language,
'I'm leaving all my little grandchildren.
I'm leaving them.'

THREE

Muleemah

One time all our people travelled
from Wallaga Lake to Bermagui to play cricket.
Uncle Abraham was the last one to arrive.

While he was travelling he saw a woman on the road.
This woman was a *muleemah*,
a man dressed in women's clothes.

MULEEMAH

Uncle Abraham said to himself,
'It's a *bugeen*.'

He goes round the back of this *muleemah*
and comes out onto the road again.
As he is walking along the road
he sees this *muleemah* again in front of him
walking along in women's clothes.
Again Uncle Abraham goes round
and gets past this *muleemah*.
When he gets to Bermagui he tells everyone
that he was caught by a *muleemah*.

Uncle Abraham plays cricket
and his side wins the game.
Then they all go back to Wallaga Lake.

There Uncle Abraham gets sick.

F O U R

Doonoots

Old Jacky (Mumbulla, my father) travels
with Uncle Abraham to Mosquito Point,
the two old-men put up their camp there.
Old Jacky makes a fire and all the *doonoots*,
the mopokes, call out:
    No sleep, no smoke,
    no sleep, no smoke,
    gook-gook, gook-gook.

The *doonoots* were calling out
and killing Uncle Abraham.
They were tying up his guts.
The old-man was dying.

Old Jacky put more wood on the fire
but the mopokes flew up
and perched on the camp-poles.
    Gook-gook, gook-gook,
    no sleep, no smoke,
    gook-gook, gook-gook,
they called out.

◆ DOONOOTS ◆

Old Jacky grabbed the fire-sticks
and pelted them at the mopokes.
He knocked one of the birds
down from the camp-poles.
He picked the mopoke up
and chucked him in the fire to burn alive
and to stop the mopokes
from killing the old feller.

But all night until daylight
the *doonoots* sing out:
    Gook-gook, gook-gook,
    no sleep, no smoke,
    gook-gook, gook-gook.

◆ Doonoots ◆

When daylight comes the poor old-man had passed away in the mia-mia camp. They took him away and buried him and saw him no more.

BIOGRAPHIES

Bronwyn Bancroft

Bronwyn Bancroft is a descendant of the Bunjalung people and she grew up in Tenterfield, NSW. Her work is represented in galleries internationally and throughout Australia. Bronwyn lives near Grafton with her children, Jack and Ella.

Bronwyn's paintings can be described as contemporary as well as Aboriginal images to which her choice of bright colours combined with her technique attest. Bronwyn has illustrated *Dirrangun* as well as Oodgeroo's *Stradbroke Dreamtime*. These illustrations have received worldwide attention and were described in the CBC *1993 Notable Books* as providing 'a modern context through which the spirit and spirituality of the stories echo with the power of authenticity.' Bronwyn was selected as the Australian candidate for the 1994 UNICEF-Ezra Jack Keats International Award for Excellence in Children's Book Illustration for her illustrations in *Stradbroke Dreamtime*.

Bronwyn also illustrated Diana Kidd's celebrated *Fat and Juicy Place* which was shortlisted in the Children's Book Council 1993 Book of the Year Awards for Younger Readers and the winner of the Australian Multicultural Children's Book Award.

Roland Robinson

Roland Robinson spent much of his life travelling in outback Australia, writing poetry and collecting Aboriginal myths, legends, and songs. In 1988 he was awarded the Patrick White Award in recognition of his life's work in literature.

Roland believed that the Aboriginal storytellers with whom he spoke during his lifetime, spoke with a rhythm that transcribed as poetry and narratives in English. Subsequently he went to great lengths to scribe accurately, making only minor punctuation changes. He also retained some words in the original language where precise translations were not possible. Variations in pronunciation were also recorded and faithful to oral tradition, Robinson scribed phonetically.

A well-respected storyteller himself, Roland published numerous collections of poetry and Aboriginal stories. Among these were *The Feathered Serpent* and *The Nearest the White Man Gets*. Roland Robinson died in 1992 and is fondly remembered.

Percy Mumbulla

Born at Wallaga Lake in the early part of the century, Percy Mumbulla was a well-known and respected storyteller. His parents, known as King Jack and Queen Rosie, represented all of the traditional ways.

Percy Mumbulla was very active in the struggle for land rights in NSW. Starting in the 1960s, until the Land Rights Bill was passed in 1983, Percy gave rousing speeches to his fellow demonstrators. His ability to rally flagging spirits was as renowned as his storytelling.

A great friendship developed between Roland Robinson, the travelling poet, and Percy over many years. Percy related his stories to Roland in the 1940s and 1950s. They were published in a number of volumes including *Black-Feller, White-Feller* and *The Nearest the White Man Gets*.

Everyone who knew Percy had a story to tell about him. Percy's love of the bush and the ocean was legendary. As an elder of his people and an expert on bush medicine, Percy would take any opportunity to return to the bush. He was also an excellent fisherman.

Percy Mumbulla died in 1991.